Memory Palace: Remember Anything and Everything

by Think like Sherlock

Copyright © 2015 by Think like Sherlock

All rights reserved. This book or any portion thereof may not be reproduced or used in any manner whatsoever without the express written permission of the publisher except for the use of brief quotations in a book review.

Printed in the United States of America

ISBN: 978-1523312887

Table of Contents

Page 1 | Introduction

Page 5 | What are you capable of?

Page 10 | What is mnemonic device?

Page 13 | Meet the Memory Palace or Method of Loci

Page 17 | Memorizing a simple shopping list

Page 24 | Memorizing a shuffled deck of cards

Page 29 | Memorizing digits

Page 38 | Learning a new language more efficiently

Page 43 | How to remember what you read?

Page 50 | Is it possible to remember what you've forgot?

Page 53 | The Final Exam

*"Memory is the treasury
and guardian of all things."*

— Marcus Tullius Cicero

1 | Memory Palace: Remember Anything and Everything

Introduction

Do you think your memory is pretty good? Then stop reading and think for a minute. What did you forget today? You would tell me, but you forgot it?

Don't worry, forgetting is a part of being human. We all forget something important, no matter how young we are.

None of us have a perfect memory because memory is too quirky, complicated, and unreliable.

In order to understand this, let's examine the main principles of memory.

How our brain works?

Every piece of an information you learn is immediately stored in your "temporary" storage – i.e. your short-term memory, also known as your working memory. It's a place which allows recall for a very short period of time. Then you can dismiss the information or transfer it to a long-term memory, which is responsible for storing, managing, and retrieving information.

There you can store much larger amounts of information for potentially unlimited duration. Its capacity, actually, is immeasurably large.

Why do we forget?

Forgetting can be explained by using the theories of trace decay, displacement, interference and lack of consolidation. When we learn something new, a neurochemical memory trace is created and over time this trace slowly disintegrates. If you don't consolidate it and transfer it to a long-term memory, it will simply disappear. It's obvious - once a memory is created, it must be properly stored.

Training your memory

These days, memory fitness is a hot topic for absolutely everyone. There's even a World Memory Championship competition, where competitors have to memorize as much information as possible within a given period of time.

Using memory techniques, most of us have the potential to become "memory champions". I have no doubt that you will be amazed how easily you can boost your memory power. Forget what others say about your age, you are never too young nor too old to acquire these skills! Memory is a faculty that's always improved by practicing.

4 | Memory Palace: Remember Anything and Everything

In this book, you will learn not only how to memorize particular types of information, but how to sharpen your memory in general.

Let the journey begin!

5 | Memory Palace: Remember Anything and Everything

What are you capable of?

We have all heard that the human brain is amazingly powerful, but most of us aren't aware of how much the mind is really capable of or what it can actually do.

You use your brain every day and you think that you know your capabilities?

Actually, not at all.

There are a number of misconceptions that people accept as true.

The truth behind most common brain and memory myths

- Having a bigger brain **doesn't** make you smarter. Even Albert Einstein had a relatively small brain!
- You **can't** use 100 % of your brain; you're already using it! There is no hidden, extra potential you can tap into. Most of your brain is active all the time, even when you're asleep.
- Hypnosis **can't** retrieve forgotten memories.
- There's **no** secret way to a good memory.

But most of these motivational speakers were right - you really are capable of amazing things. Your brain is very flexible and can become much more powerful through deliberate training!

7 | Memory Palace: Remember Anything and Everything

The same applies to memory. There is no secret way to a brilliant memory, but you can memorize a huge amount of information using special techniques.

In order to prove it, here are some official records from World Memory Championship:

- **Speed cards** - Simon Reinhard from Germany managed to recall as single deck of 52 cards in 21.19 seconds.

- **Spoken numbers** - Jonas von Essen from Sweden remembered 380 digits.

- **Hour cards** - Ben Pridmore from Nottinghamshire in the UK holds the title for remembering 28 decks of 1,456 cards in an hour.

- **Binary numbers** - Ben Pridmore managed to recall 4,140 digits of binary numbers - strings of numbers consisting of 1 and 0 in 30 minutes.

- **Names and faces** - a second achievement for Simon Reinhard is that he matched and remembered 186 names and faces.

- **Hour numbers** - Wang Feng from China holds the record for the most random digits, in rows of 40, remembered in an hour

- **Random words** – Here we have another appearance for Germany's Simon Reinhard who holds the record for 300 random words recounted in 15 minutes

- **Historical dates** - Johannes Mallow holds the title for remembering 132 dates and the events they are linked to in five minutes

- **Abstract images** - Mallow also is the champion of abstract images, after recalling 492 pictures in sequence in 15 minutes

- **Speed numbers** – Mallow further holds a joint record for remembering 501 numbers in rows of 40 in five minutes

Amazing, right?

9 | Memory Palace: Remember Anything and Everything

And I actually know what you're thinking. I can assure you that these individuals are not super humans, and they don't have any superpowers. They just learned how to use memory techniques, also known as mnemonic devices.

What is mnemonic device?

Mnemonic device is a technique you can use to improve your ability to remember something. Mnemonics help learners to recall large pieces of information, like steps, parts, stages or phases with a 100% accuracy.

In other words, it's a memory technique to help your brain better systemize, encode and recall information. It's a shortcut that helps you associate the information you want to remember with an image, a sentence, or a word.

11 | Memory Palace: Remember Anything and Everything

In this century, one of the most analyzed and brilliant memories belongs to Russian journalist and professional mnemonist Solomon Shereshevsky. According to neuropsychologist Alexander Luria, who studied Shereshevsky for thirty years, there were no distinct limits to his memory. As a journalist, Shereshevsky never took notes during the interviews, but all of his articles were very detailed and accurate. He told the editor that he didn't need to take notes, because he never forgot anything!

Like the most memory wizards, Shereshevsky had his own unique mnemonic system. Luria discovered that he had an ability called synesthesia, which involved all of his senses in remembering something.

If he heard music, the notes triggered flashes of color. If he touched something, it caused him to experience taste. He could memorize a poem in a foreign language by linking the words to similar sounds in Russian, even if they had different meanings.

These days, many are using these systems. It's the best way of memorizing information and "sticking" it within your brain longer for easy recall in the future.

In 1967, a study by Gerald R. Miller showed that mnemonics really increases recall. He found out that students who regularly used mnemonic devices, increased their test scores up to 77%!

Some of the mnemonic devices date back to ancient Greek times. This book is dedicated to one of the most popular mnemonic devices, adopted in ancient Roman and Greek rhetorical treatises - the Memory Palace, also known as Method of Loci.

Meet the Memory Palace or Method of Loci

The Method of Loci is the oldest known mnemonic system. It has been used since ancient times to easily memorize speeches and other important information.

The system is based on the assumption that you can best remember places that you're familiar with. You just need to link the information with a place that you know very well and it will serve as a clue that will help you to remember.

According to Cicero in his Rhetorica ad Herenium, the system was developed by the poet Simonides of Ceos, who was the only survivor of a building collapse during a dinner. Simonides easily identified everyone who were missing or dead by remembering where the guests had been sitting.

The Memory Palace was used by both Greek and Roman orators, who were able to give speeches without the aid of notes. This system gives the best results if you're good at visualizing things.

How to use it?

To use the Method of Loci, you need to associate things you wish to remember with locations of a familiar room, building or street. Then, to retrieve the information, you simply need to take a walk through the location and the images will pop in your mind immediately.

To make it more effective, you must visualize an object doing something at a particular location.

Let's build it...

Think of a place you know very well.

For the first time, I recommend you use the path through your own house.

Now you need to divide the path to a particular locations.

For our first exercise, we will need 10 of them. Imagine your usual way to your room when you get home. As you enter each of them, move logically in the same direction, from one side of the room to the other.

Keep in mind that you must take the same route through your house each time, otherwise you'll likely get a mental block.

You've already finished? Let's get it to practice!

17 | Memory Palace: Remember Anything and Everything

Memorizing a simple shopping list

Here's a simple shopping list for you:

- Tomatoes
- Tea
- Light bulb
- Milk
- Eggs
- Wine
- Soap
- Scissors
- Toothpaste
- Ice cream

18 | Memory Palace: Remember Anything and Everything

Try to memorize this list by placing each item that you want to remember at one of the locations.

Here's an example on placing the items:

1. Tomatoes

As you visualize a front door of your house, imagine someone throwing tomatoes at it. You need to form vivid images, so don't just visualize it, try to feel it, use all your senses. You can imagine that some of the juice has been spattered on your clothes.

2. Tea

As you step into your house, imagine that you've accidentally spilled a tea on the sofa.

3. Lightbulb

Imagine a huge lightbulb sitting in the armchair. The more absurd images you create, the easier it is to remember them.

4. Milk

Imagine a cow standing on your desk.

5. Eggs
Imagine a whole bed covered by eggs or a big chicken sleeping in it.

6. Wine
Imagine a pot of wine boiling on the cooker. Try to feel the taste or smell of it.

7. Soap
Imagine a huge soap bar sitting on your sink and washing your dishes.

8. Scissors
Imagine a giant scissors cutting your dining table.

9. Toothpaste
Imagine someone squeezing a toothpaste in the toilet.

10. Ice Cream
Imagine a full bath of ice cream. Feel the cold of it.

21 | MEMORY PALACE: REMEMBER ANYTHING AND EVERYTHING

Once you've finished placing all your list items around the house, simply start again from the front door. You will instantly see tomatoes on the door, tea on the sofa and so on. Keep in mind that the more unusual the images are, the easier it is to remember them.

After you get familiar with the system, you can build much bigger and more powerful palaces, like a familiar street in your neighborhood, your school, your place of work, or even a mall.

Some memory championship competitors use their childhood homes. It's up to you how much of them you will have in your head.

Now try it yourself:

Grocery list:

- Onions
- Cherries
- Pizza
- Honey
- Pasta
- Olives
- Salt
- Salmon
- Juice
- Batteries

To-do list:

- Read a book
- Wish your mother/father happy birthday
- Pay bills
- Wash car
- Get laundry
- Buy groceries
- Call your local post office

- Check your email
- Dye your hair
- Start learning Spanish

Actually, I don't recommend memorizing your to-do lists. It's more effective to write them down somewhere and work through it systematically. If you will keep them in mind, there's a chance that you'll simply forget what you need to do. But this time it will be a good exercise for you. Be sure to form unusual images that will stick instantly.

Memorizing a shuffled deck of cards

One of the most exciting things I've ever seen is memorizing a shuffled deck of cards. It is a good way to impress your friends, it could be used in the card games also. But please, don't cheat! You know that everyone hates cheaters!

In this chapter, I'll show you how to combine 52 unconnected pieces of data together and memorize a whole deck of playing cards in a few minutes. As I mentioned before, Simon Reinhard from

Germany managed to recall as single deck in 21.19 seconds. Maybe you'll be the new world record holder?

This time you'll need to expand your memory palace to 52 places.

Personally I like to use Grandmaster's of Memory Ed Cooke's technique, in which you have to convert 52 cards into 52 celebrities. To make it easier, each suit corresponds to a personality type and each card corresponds to a profession.

The suits looks like this:

♦ – rich people,

♥ – people you love,

♣ – tough or crazy people,

♠ – amusing or absurd people.

Let's dive into a cards:

Kings and Queens stands for celebrity couples. Each suit will have its own couple. Jacks – religious figures.

10's are powerful women,
9's are powerful men,
8's are famous female physiques, bodies of your dreams,
7's are famous male physicists,
6's are controversial females,
5's are controversial males,
4's are female movie stars,
3's are male movie stars,
2's are sportswomen,
Aces are sportsmen.

You need to learn only 17 things – 13 professions and 4 personalities and now

27 | Memory Palace: Remember Anything and Everything

it's up to you how you fill out a 52-card matrix.

Here's my example with hearts – lovely people:

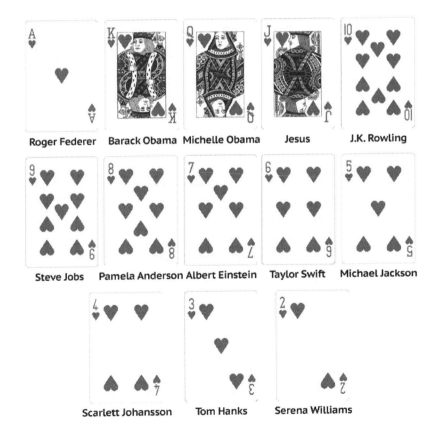

Using this method, in less than an hour, you'll be able to slowly recall the people corresponding to the cards. When starting to place them in your memory palace, keep it simple, because using a longer path with multiple points per room will cause you an overload. Take your time to imagine each celebrity vividly in their position.

After you've finished the deck, retrace it in your head and fill the missing gaps. You will probably need to go through it 2 or 3 times on the first attempt, but you will be amazed when the images will pop into your head instantly.

Now grab a shuffled deck of cards and start translating the cards to their images until it's automatic!

Memorizing digits

There's a lot numbers around us every day. We have to remember telephone numbers, PIN codes, passwords, birthdays and all sorts of numbers, but unfortunately, our brain are notoriously poor at memorizing them.

The main problem is that numbers, represented visually by symbols, still are abstract concepts and don't feel very appealing to our brains.

This time you will meet the Major memory system – one of the most powerful techniques for memorizing sequences of numbers.

The system is converting abstract, dull numbers into vivid images for easy memorizing.

It often forms the basis of some of the extraordinary memory feats performed by magicians and memory performers.

It takes some time to master it, but once learned, it could be a very good friend in your everyday life.

The core of the Major system is a 10-item mnemonic table, which shows how to transform the digits 0 to 9 into corresponding sounds, which we will use to form words.

Take a look at it:

31 | Memory Palace: Remember Anything and Everything

Number	Sound	How to memorize it
0	s, z, soft c	z is the first letter of zero, others have similar sound
1	t, d, th	t & d have one downstroke and sound similar
2	n	n has two downstrokes
3	m	m has three downstrokes and looks like a 3 on it's side
4	r	r is the last letter of four
5	l	L is the Roman Numeral for 50
6	j, sh, soft ch, dg, zh, soft g	a script j has a lower loop and g is almost a 6 rotated. These letters also have a 'whistle-like' sound, and 6 looks like a whistle
7	k, hard c, hard g, q, qu	capital K contains two 7s (on their sides, back to back)
8	v, f	think of v as in a V8 motor. f sounds similar (notice how your teeth touch your lips for both)
9	b, p	p is a mirror-image 9. b sounds similar and resembles a 9 rolled around
-	vowel sounds, w, h, y	These can be used anywhere without changing a word's number value

For example, let's decode the number 13. According to the table, digits 1 and 3 translates to *t* and *m*. Now we need to form a word with these letters. For me, the word *time* looks best in this situation. We filled the gaps between the letters with vowels *i* and *e*. You can use the neutral *w, h,* and *y* to form the word, but I don't think that there's a simpler version for it than *time*.

The conversion may seem a little slow at first, but practice makes perfect.

It's important to choose the words which are easy to visualize. Concrete nouns always work better than abstract ones. I don't recommend using adjectives or verbs too.

Let's take it to practice:

We need to memorize 8-digit phone number: **1876-3347.**

33 | Memory Palace: Remember Anything and Everything

Let's start by dividing the number to pairs. It looks like this: 18 | 76 | 33 | 47.
In this case, 18 translates to *d* and *v*. The word *dove* immediately pops into my mind.

76 translates to *cage*, 33 to *mummy* and 47 to *rock*.

At the end, we have a four words: *dove*, *cage*, *mummy* and *rock*. They will require only four locations in your memory palace.

Let's start placing them there: imagine a huge dove flying around you as you enter your house. The door behind your back suddenly closes, you look around and realize that you're trapped in a cage. There's a bars around you and the mummy appears as you enter your living room. You try to reach it, but a huge rock just drops on your feet.

Congratulations, you memorized your first phone number! This time I've made it simple, but you can form more ridiculous, funny images for guaranteed memorizing.

If translating the letters to words looks too hard for you, Litemind.com created a table of translations from 0 to 99:

0. Sow
1. Hat
2. Hen
3. Ham
4. Row
5. Hill
6. Shoe
7. Cow
8. Ivy
9. Bee
10. Toes
11. Dad
12. Dune
13. Dime
14. Tire
15. Doll
16. Tissue
17. Duck
18. Dove
19. Tape
20. Nose
21. Net
22. Nun
23. Nemo
24. Nero
25. Nail
26. Notch
27. Neck
28. Knife
29. Knob
30. Mouse
31. Mat

Memory Palace: Remember Anything and Everything

32. Moon
33. Mummy
34. Mower
35. Mule
36. Match
37. Mug
38. Movie
39. Map
40. Rose
41. Road
42. Rain
43. Room
44. Aurora
45. Rail
46. Rash
47. Rock
48. Roof
49. Rope
50. Lace
51. Loot
52. Lion
53. Lime
54. Lure
55. Lily
56. Leech
57. Log
58. Lava
59. Lip
60. Cheese
61. Sheet
62. Chain
63. Jam
64. Cherry
65. Jello
66. Judge
67. Chalk
68. Chef
69. Ship
70. Gas
71. Cat
72. Can
73. Comb
74. Car
75. Coal
76. Cage
77. Coke

78. Cave	94. Bear
79. Cape	95. Bell
80. Fez	96. Bush
81. Fat	97. Book
82. Fan	98. Beef
83. Foam	99. Pipe
84. Fire	00. S.O.S.
85. File	01. Seed
86. Fish	02. Sun
87. Fog	03. Sam
88. Fife	04. Zero
89. Fib	05. Seal
90. Bus	06. Sash
91. Bat	07. Sack
92. Pen	08. Sofa
93. Opium	09. Sepia

You can link the numbers with your additional memory palaces you've created. If you need to memorize your friend's telephone number, place the things in his house; if you need to memorize barber's number, place the things in the barbershop.

Memory Palace: Remember Anything and Everything

Your imagination is unlimited, so don't be afraid to use it!

Want to practice? Here are some fake numbers:

- 1559-6082
- 4505-6150
- 5230-1721
- 8236-5244
- 6034-1166
- 2714-8641
- 8810-6410
- 6562-7164

Learning a new language more efficiently

Let's say that for some reason you decided to learn a new language. How much time you think you need to spend to become a fluent speaker? 5, 6 years? No!

As Benny Lewis, the author of *Fluent in 3 Months: How Anyone at Any Age Can Learn to Speak Any Language from Anywhere in the World* says, you can become fluent in 3 months! And it's true, actually.

Using the proper effective learning techniques and avoiding the main mistakes you can become a polyglot in a very short period of time.

Learning a new language is exciting and beneficial at all ages. Whatever your age, being bilingual has its advantages, especially in today's global society.

Medical studies has shown the positive effects learning a new language has on the brain. Learning significantly delayed the onset of many brain diseases, such as Alzheimer and dementia. Despite advantages for the brain, being bilingual opens up a world of new opportunities, job prospects, understanding of other cultures.

If you'll get familiar with mnemonic techniques for learning the languages more efficiently, you'll be able to forget the embarrassment when you need to spend a long time on flicking through a phrase book whenever you need to say something in the shop, bar or any other public places.

You will master the basics of any language that you choose in a very short period of time. Forget cramming and don't punish yourself with it anymore.

The system works by transforming a foreign words into a form that is instantly understandable and memorable.

If you want to commit a word to your long-term memory with easy recall, the first thing you need to do is convert it into a form that you can immediately visualize.

For example, let's take the Spanish word *dinero*, which means *money*. At first sight. it looks like a bunch of syllables and it's difficult to visualise. But if we try to pronounce it, we are actually able to break this word into the two distinct sounds, *the-narrow*.

41 | Memory Palace: Remember Anything and Everything

You've successfully transformed a meaningless collection of syllables into two meaningful words! Now we need to link them together and associate with English word *money*. For example, you can visualize that you've picked up a coin from your pocket and it immediately started to narrow.

Be sure to visualize it vividly. I'm absolutely sure that now you don't have any difficulties in remembering the meaning of *dinero*!

Here's another example with a French word *chou*, which means *cabbage* in English. This word is pronounced like *shoe* in English, so it's very simple - imagine yourself putting on cabbages on your feet instead of shoes.

French word *van*, which means *wine*, can be easily remember by visualizing a large van, which is crammed full with crates of the wine. However, the mnemonics are more effective if you create them yourself.

The method that I've shown you looks a little bit long and hard but -- as I mentioned before – practice makes perfect! After a while, you will develop the ability to transform foreign words to images instantly – as soon as you hear a new word.

Basically, the vividness and absurdity of an image makes it memorable. That's why your old textbooks were so hard to digest!
Don't procrastinate anymore and start learning a new language. It's an awesome exercise for brain and enormous boost of self-confidence when you can speak in other languages!

How to remember what you read

Despite the age of technologies, you spend a good part of your day reading something. You're reading newspapers to catch up with what's going on in the world, you read books, letters, or just any kind of stuff that media presents us.

You've learned to read when you were a kid and it seems that, surely, you must be a good reader?
Not at all. One of the main reasons that people don't read much is that they don't how to do it

properly. For example, most of the students has to read something several times before they understand and remember it.

How many times you were desperate for some book on a subject you were eager to learn about and at the end, you realized that you were no more knowledgeable than you were when you started?

You can become more efficient reader and still understand what you're reading by following these simple steps:

1. **Read on purpose**

OK, you've picked up your next book to read. Now think, why do you want to read it?

What's your purpose to do this?

Maybe you need to write a report about, maybe you're just interested in the particular subject? Anyway, ask yourself "why I read this?" and when you consciously know the reason for choosing this book, write it somewhere.

Now you have the directions on what you need to focus on and what you can ignore.

2. Skim through your book before reading

Let's face it: Like most people, you grab a new book and start reading from the first sentence. But most of your reading tasks actually require no more than skimming.

Instead of wasting your time, it's more effective to check out the headings, pictures, tables and other things first.

Most of the books have the main points described at the end of the chapter, so take a look at them and try to figure what they will teach you.

You should slow down and read carefully only the parts, which is fulfilling the reading purpose.

The main benefits of the skimming is:

1. It leaves a trace on your memory, making it easier to remember when you read it the second time.
2. It gives you some orientation, helping you know where the most important content is.
3. It gives you an overall sense of the structure, which makes it easier to remember certain parts.

Start using this advice and you will be a step forward to a faster and efficient reading.

3. Eliminate all distractions

Concentration is the main factor of good memorization. If you don't concentrate on what you read, you will simply waste your time.

Be sure to eliminate all distractions around you and make yourself comfortable.

4. Start taking notes

Get familiar with note taking. You can write the things down in your notes, or you can highlight them in the book.
Most of the students are using highlighters for the main things in the text. But the problem is that they highlight too much of the text or they highlight the wrong things.
I recommend you read a whole chapter and only then, after a short break (a few minutes), skip through the text and highlight or write down the most important things in the text that you've noticed. It will be a good rehearsal for you too.

5. Rehearse, rehearse, rehearse!

If it's a study material, you'll definitely need to rehearse it.

Here's how to use your study time effectively:

- Divide your study time into a 1-hour segments.
- After each of them, take a 10 minute break and run through the material you've been studying or check out your notes for a 5 minute period.

If you want to transfer the information to a long-term memory more effectively, follow this rehearsal timeline:

- Next day after learning, you have to study your notes for 2-4 minutes.
- After a week, 2 minutes will be enough to trigger your memories.
- After a month, the same 2 minutes applies.

For this kind of rehearsal, the mind mapping technique works best. It's really worth checking out.

After using these methods, you will see an immediate results on easier reading and better recalling. Good luck!

Is it possible to remember what you've forgot?

How many times did you find yourself in the situation when you want to remember something? You have it on the tip of your tongue, but even if you try to do that, you won't achieve anything? Or you find yourself in a room with no idea what you came there to do?

Luckily, you're not the only one with this kind of problem. Sometimes our brain just slips-up on remembering even the simplest things.

We can't do anything about it, that's the way it works. Try not to blame it and use the following steps.

I have no idea what I'm here for!

Admit it, everyone experienced that feeling when you thought about something in one place, and, as you entered another, it slipped out of your mind.

Research has shown that people are better at remembering things in an environment matching the environment where it was learned.

If you thought about something in the bedroom and forgot it when you got to the living room, go back to the bedroom.

The familiar environment will be a very powerful trigger and possibly help you retrieve the forgotten information.

It's on the tip of my tongue...

If you're having problems on remembering something, don't panic and make the first step – relax. Anxiety blocks your ability to remember even the simplest things.

- Try to recreate the possible environmental triggers. Maybe you were listening to a particular song or watching a TV show when you've thought about it? Try using them!
- Stop focusing on the thing that you want to remember and think about something else. The memory possibly will come back naturally.

Try to reconstruct the scene when you've thought about something. Use all your senses. Try imagining where you were and what you were doing. Just reconstruct the whole scenario.

The Final Exam

Ready to take the final exam? Without going back, test your memorizing skills and write down your scores:

15 random words

- Cat
- Snake
- Table
- Bicycle
- Banana
- Frog
- Field

- Book
- Sunglasses
- Keys
- Brain
- Socks
- Pistol
- Basket
- Calculator

Score: _/15

5 Telephone Numbers

1. 5418-8489
2. 2214-5789
3. 3569-4654
4. 6468-9221
5. 9849-1561

Score: _/5

55 | Memory Palace: Remember Anything and Everything

Sequence of 15 playing cards

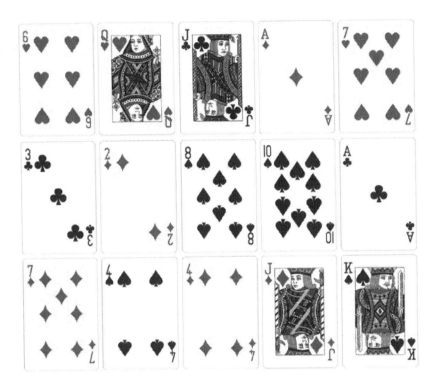

Score: __/15

Total score: __/35

Final word

Congratulations on your first huge step to a brilliant memory.

As you see, it's not as hard as it looks. You just need to practice every day for the best results. Now, when you've got a good sense of the mnemonic things, you can start creating them yourself! But don't forget – absurdity and vivid images will always stick better than the dull ones!

Before you leave...

Your opinion is very important to me. Please take few seconds to post a review on Amazon.

Made in the USA
Middletown, DE
25 May 2016